ASKA'S BIRDS

Paintings by Warabé Aska   *Poetry by David Day*

A Doubleday Book for Young Readers

A Doubleday Book for Young Readers

Published in Canada by Doubleday Canada Limited,
105 Bond Street, Toronto, Ontario, Canada, M5B 1Y3.

Published in the USA by Delacorte Press,
Bantam Doubleday Dell Publishing Group, Inc.,
666 Fifth Avenue,
New York, New York, 10103.

Canadian Cataloguing in Publication Data

Aska, Warabé
Aska's birds

Poems.
ISBN 0-385-25388-5

1. Aska, Warabé. 2. Birds in art. I. Day, David, 1947– . II. Title.

ND249.A84A4 1992 704.9'43 C92–094051-X

Library of Congress Cataloging-in-Publication data applied for
ISBN 0-385-25388-5

Design by Ross Mah Design Associates
Printed and bound in Hong Kong
1992 Canada / 1993 U.S.A.
10 9 8 7 6 5 4 3 2 1

If birds were people, what jobs would they do? It's a

PELICANS

Pelicans are feathered fishermen,
Who open their gaping nets
To gather a slippery harvest.
They dream of a glorious heaven
Where every cloud has a fishy, silvery lining.

Title page:

guessing game for me and you.

If ducks were people, what jobs would they do? It's a guessing game for me and you. It's a guessing

DUCKS

Dutifully, the duck drills the dawdling ducklings.
She is the schoolmistress on a class outing.
Step by staggering step, stroke by unsteady stroke,
Her fledglings learn to make their way.

If woodpeckers were people, what jobs would they do? It's a guessing game for me and you. It's a

WOODPECKER

The forest drummer beats and beats on his wooden drum,
His head aglow with the red-hot news.
A flurry of wings. A peal of laughter.
Then the "rat-a-tat-tat" of the woodpecker's tattoo.

If parrots were people, what jobs would they do? It's a guessing game for me and you. It's a guess

PARROT

The parrot becomes a feathered rainbow in flight,
A screech of gaudy color arching through the tropic sky.
He is the forest clown and mimic,
The harlequin spirit of paradise.

If penguins were people, what jobs would they do? It's a guessing game for me and you. It's a gues

PENGUINS

A patchwork of perfectly packed penguins.
An immaculate army of tuxedos in nature's icebox.
They are the unruffled headwaiters of the ice floes,
The chief butlers of the antarctic.

If ostriches were people, what jobs would they do? It's a guessing game for me and you. It's a gues

OSTRICHES

Pirouette. Pose and strut. Point to point.
The ostriches are dancers in bizarre disguise.
On a sunbaked stage,
They patiently practice their strange ballet.

If flamingos were people, what jobs would they do? It's a guessing game for me and you. It's a gue

FLAMINGOS

Flamingos are exotic twilight artists
Who create impossible sunsets.
Each evening, with long feathered wingstrokes
They paint pink the pale roof of the sky.

Warabé

If snowy egrets were people, what jobs would they do? It's a guessing game for me and you. It's a

SNOWY EGRETS

A frosting of snowy egrets settles in the treetops.
They are forest rangers standing on guard.
Should shooting stars threaten their leafy home,
They are ready to raise the alarm.

If doves were people, what jobs would they do? It's a guessing game for me and you. It's a guessi

DOVE

What is the sound of starlight?
It's the whisper of white feathers,
A lullaby from the heavens.
The dove is a storyteller whose gentle tales bring peace
To lonely nestlings in the forest of night.

If snowy owls were people, what jobs would they do? It's a guessing game for me and you. It's a g

SNOWY OWL

Who knows best the changes of the moon?
Who haunts the long dark of the arctic night?
Who is the guardian of the forest laden with snow?
Who? Who? Who?
It's the moon-eyed snowy owl,
The night watchman of the wilderness.

Warabé

If peacocks were people, what jobs would they do? It's a guessing game for me and you. It's a gues

PEACOCK

The white peacock is the proud park keeper
Strutting vainly through his wide domain.
He mists the glade like a crystal fountain,
And dusts the leaves with his plumes.

If crows were people, what jobs would they do? It's a guessing game for me and you. It's a guessin

CROWS

Who knows the dark business of crows?

They are detectives in a world of twilight and shadow.

If only we understood the gossip of crows,

We might learn where stolen jewels are hidden.

If eagles were people, what jobs would they do? It's a guessing game for me and you. It's a guessin

EAGLE

Terror crowds around the eagle,
His wings churn up a blasting wind.
His eyes are burned-out stars,
He is the bogeyman of the bird kingdom.
Fear of him makes fledglings obey mother's every command.

If swans were people, what jobs would they do? It's a guessing game for me and you. It's a guessin

SWANS

The swans are nursemaids among the rushes.
In nature's nursery
They are the guardians
Who take lost babes beneath sheltering wings.

If gulls were people, what jobs would they do? It's a guessing game for me and you. It's a guessing

GULLS

Their wings as white as the crests of the waves,
Gulls flutter and soar, as they patrol the sea.
Search and rescue teams of the wild and windy shore.

This has been a flight of fancy. Our imaginations, like birds,

were given wings.